The Oldies Music Aptitude Test

Trivia Fun for Armchair Deejays

Praise for *The Oldies Music Aptitude Test*

"If you are going to have any book on Rock 'n Roll trivia, this should be it!"

Dick Biondi, Oldies 104.3, WJMK, Chicago

"School was never this much fun! Grab your pencil and get set for a blast through the past!"

Brian Beirne, "Mr. Rock 'n Roll,"
Oldies Radio 101, K-EARTH, Los Angeles

"Wow! 'The Oldies Music Aptitude Test' is the most fun exam I've ever taken. Anyone who grew up in the golden age of Rock 'n Roll will not be able to put this book down!"

Bob Walker, "The Oldie King,"
Oldies KOOL-95.5, New Orleans

"What a lot of fun! Great categories and creative questions make this a must-have for those who think they know it all!"

Kitty Loewry, Oldies CD-94.7, Chicago

"'The Oldies Music Aptitude Test' is a funny and fun look back at the music our generation grew up with. Great work!"

Jim Johnson, WCSX-FM, Detroit

"A wonderful collection of rock 'n roll questions... I especially got a kick out of the fascinating classifications."

Dusty Rhodes, WGRR, Oldies 103.5, Cincinnati

"I give 'The Oldies Music Aptitude Test' an A+! You gotta pass this rock and roll quiz if you wanna dance with me!"

Richie Rotkin, The Rip Chords ("Hey Little Cobra")

"This is the funnest test you will ever take, with entertaining and cleverly thought out categories and questions that will even make you laugh out loud. Did you ever do that when you took the S.A.T.?"

Kel Waddle, Access To The Music Zone

"What a fabulous trip down memory lane! 'The Oldies Music Aptitude Test' left me smiling and feeling warm, a wonderful trip back to the time when rock was defined!"

Brian R. Corbishley, The Extreme Trivia Challenge

"With lots of warmth and love for the songs and artists, Ms Jastrab delivers with this clever, well-written and much needed collection of oldies puzzlers that will challenge rookies and experts alike."

Ron Smith, Oldiesmusic.com

The Oldies Music Aptitude Test

Trivia Fun for Armchair Deejays

Barbara Jastrab

Writers Club Press

San Jose New York Lincoln Shanghai

The Oldies Music Aptitude Test
Trivia Fun for Armchair Deejays

Writers Club Press
an imprint of iUniverse.com, Inc.

For information address:
iUniverse.com, Inc.
620 North 48th Street, Suite 201
Lincoln, NE 68504-3467
www.iuniverse.com

Cover art and illustrations by Dominick Tucci
Foreword by Dick Biondi

ISBN: 0-595-14166-8

Printed in the United States of America

With love to the men in this little girl's life—

my sons, David and Jordan,

and my husband, Jerry…doo lang, doo lang, doo lang.

Contents

Foreword

Oldies.

That's a word which has gained new meaning over the last 25 years. It probably started with the expression, "an oldie but a goodie," perhaps having nothing to do with music. In 1961, Little Caesar and The Romans had a hit record called "Those Oldies But Goodies," and after that rock 'n roll adopted the term. Today, in the era of CDs, *any* vinyl record could probably be considered an "oldie." But, in my definition, the true meaning of "oldies" has to do with the rock 'n roll records of the late 1950s, the 1960s, and the early 1970s.

Oldies mean a lot to what's now become known as the "baby boomer" generation. But they have an even more special meaning to me. I have lived through (and worked in) both the era when oldies weren't oldies yet, and the more recent years when oldies have undergone a major resurgence as part of the culture of the latter part of the 20th century.

Deejaying at WLS in Chicago in the early sixties, I was there when "Top 40" radio really took off. Now at WJMK-FM Oldies 104.3 in Chicago for the past 15+ years, I've watched the nostalgia boom grow to where the hit music we grew up with is now everywhere. The famous 1950s cartoon showing an elderly couple of the future dancing to "Hound Dog" and saying, "They're playing our song," seemingly preposterous at the time, has come true!

And what better way to take you back to those wonderful songs of yester-year than "The Oldies Music Aptitude Test." If you are going to have any book on Rock 'n Roll trivia, this should be it! With wit and intelligence, this tuneful trivia tribute will keep diehard oldies fans entertained for hours at a time, just like the music it celebrates.

So put on your blue suede shoes or your short shorts and relive the songs of your past with your friends. It's a challenge that'll make you feel young again!

Dick Biondi
Chicago, Illinois
April, 2000

Preface

Nothing evokes the nostalgic passion of the 78 million of us who make up the Baby Boomer generation quite like the music that surrounded, shaped and marked our youth so indelibly, and we refuse to let it go. Our feet still press the gas pedal a little harder with "Born To Be Wild" on the car radio, and we smirk when a Muzak version of "Octopus' Garden" is piped into the department store elevator. To our children's horror, we not only know all the words to "American Woman," a song they know only by the '90s cover version, but we sing along—loudly!

If you share my enthusiasm for oldies music, then I hope this book will bring back warm memories of the glory days of rock and roll, when "Everyday People" wasn't just the theme song for a car commercial.

Ohhh, oldies tunes in advertisements! *That's* a good theme for the next book!

Do *you* have a theme idea? Find a mistake in the book? Want to schmooze with other oldies music lovers? Want to play my online oldies trivia games? I'd love to hear from you! You can reach me at childof60s@aol.com.

Long live rock!

Barb

Acknowledgements

I know what it's like to be frustrated by lousy trivia questions, and so with exhaustive research as the backbone of *The Oldies Music Aptitude Test*, I designed each question to evoke one and only one definitive answer. My primary reference was my now dog-eared copy of Joel Whitburn's *The Billboard Book of Top 40 Hits, 6th edition*. This work is so respected that "according to Joel…" is the final word among music trivians. Thank you Mr. Whitburn, for this argument-settling music Bible.

Ken Rapoport, John Fox and Alan Adams are three funny and brilliant men whose generosity in time, humor, and constructive criticism over several years of manuscript revisions significantly improved the book's "fun quotient" and precision. I am honored to call them my friends. Thanks, guys!

I was also extremely fortunate to have Doug Stitt and Melissa Vaughan, two astounding rock trivians, among my later proof-readers. They picked up small inconsistencies which would have certainly undermined the accuracy of this book. Thanks so much!

My gratitude also to Robert Nash for his macabre sense of humor and help in penning the "Tragedy Songs" game. You are a sick puppy, Yank!

To the "quirky" Lisa Mos, for helping me find the perfect words for word-less concepts and untangling my awkward phrasing, many thanks!

To the positively awesome Ron Hontz and Wayne Garvin, lyrics gurus of the internet…without your qualitative transcriptions, there'd simply be no *Oldies Music Aptitude Test*.

Teri Elias, Karen Sirois and Mike Parks, your help in connecting me with the right people at the right time was invaluable! Thank you!

Most importantly…deepest gratitude to the regular players of "Classic Rock Jukebox." The ultimate compliment one can pay a host is to become a regular. Your enthusiasm and loyalty are my inspiration each week. Special thanks to Roxanne Brown, who has *never* missed one of my games! Thank you all for making Wednesday nights so rewarding and fun for so many years!

—BBJ

Introduction

What is "The Oldies Music Aptitude Test"?

If you came of age during The Sixties or Seventies, what do you remember most from your high school days?

Math? Uh-uh. Science? No way! History? Oh please, you're kidding, right?

The only thing that really mattered was…rock 'n roll.

Oh, you couldn't simply listen to rock…no, it had to be experienced!

Each morning, you tuned into your favorite AM radio station to find out which record topped the charts. You belted out "Ain't Too Proud To Beg" during your shower, maybe even trying a Temptations step or two. You found yourself humming Sam Cooke's "Wonderful World" during History class. Over lunch, you and your buddies discussed the British Invasion act on last night's Ed Sullivan Show. Before tackling your homework, you stacked the record player high with 45s. With your transistor radio's earphone in place, your last thought before sleep was puzzling over the lyrics of "A Whiter Shade of Pale."

Nice memories there.

But recall also those dark winter Saturday mornings reporting to your high school gym to take the S.A.T., where just last week at the dance you played air guitar to "Louie Louie." Your eyes glued to the clock, stomach churning in anticipation, you finger your pocketful of #2 pencils until at the appointed time the proctor pronounces the rules for the next three excruciating hours:

"Mark only within the oval…social security number…college code…blah blah blah…"

No…not such a nice memory there.

> *Now, if colleges wanted a true measure of what you learned during high school, it would be the test you hold in your hands: 600 questions on your knowledge of rock 'n roll!*

As for the serious sounding test categories you'll find within…well, that's just to poke a bit of fun at our friends in Princeton. And best of all, there are no time limits, no stop signs to prevent you from moving onto the next section, no seals to break "with the eraser end of your #2 pencil," heck, no #2 pencils at all for that matter! Go ahead, go wild, use a pen!

When you've completed all the tests, use the Final Score Interpretation to see how your rock acumen rates!

Good luck, have fun, and remember: *Rock and Roll is here to PLAY!*

Test One

Language Arts

FOREIGN LANGUAGE—*Nonsense lyrics*

> **Name the Top 40 song in which you would hear the following nonsense lyrics.**
>
> **One point for each correct song title.**

1. "A wop bop a loo bop, a lop bam boom!" ✓

2. "Boom! Shaka-laka-laka. Boom! Shaka-laka-laka" ✓

3. "Gliddy glup gloopy, nibby nabby noopy, la la la lo lo"

4. "Lie-la-lie, lielielielielielielie, lie-la-lie"

5. "Doo lang doo lang doo lang" ✓

6. "Ooga chaka, ooga ooga ooga chaka"

7. "Getcha getcha ya ya da da, getcha getcha ya ya here" ✓

8. "Toot toot! Awww, beep beep!" ✓

9. "Oo-ee, oo-ee baby, oo-ee, oo-ee baby"

10. "Tweedely-deedely-dee" ✓

11. "Oo-ee, oo-ah-ah, ting, tang, walla walla bing bang"

12. "Bo bick, bananafana fo fick, fee fi mo mick" ✓

3

13.   "Ho-voh-dee-oh-doe"

14.   "A-wim-o-weh, a-wim-o-weh, a-wim-o-weh, a-wim-o-weh" ✓

15.   "Come-a come-a down, doobie doo down down"

16.   "Doo-wop, diddy-wop, diddy-wop-doo. Doo-wop, diddy-wop, diddy-wop-doo"

17.   "Ba-yip-yip-yip-yip-yip-yip-yip-yip, boom-boom-boom-boom-boom-boom"

/ 18.   "Bom bidda-bom-bom-bom-bom-bom-bom, bidda, bom bidda-bom, a dang-a-dang-dang, a-dinga-dong-ding"

19.   "Bon c'est bon, bon bon c'est bon bon, bon c'est bon bon bon bon bon"

20.   "Roly poly, roly poly, roly poly poly"

(Answer key on page 83)

"I read the news today, oh boy"

JOURNALISM—*Tragedy Songs*

> **Name the Top 40 song described by each of the following tragic newspaper headlines.**
>
> **One point for each correct song title.**

1. *Teenage Girl Dies In Car-Train Crash While Retrieving High School Ring*

2. *Enraged Man Stabs Unfaithful Lover To Death*

3. *Teen Leaps From County Bridge Under Mysterious Circumstances* ✓

4. *All Hands Lost In Lake Superior Shipping Disaster*

5. *National Guard Guns Down Kent State Four* ✓

6. *Officials Fear Worst As All Contact Lost With Astronaut*

7. *Young Bride Dies After Planting Tree*

8. *Special Forces Soldier Killed In Vietnam While Young Wife Waits*

9. *Large Man Dies In Mine In Act Of Heroism*

10. *Rookie Race Driver Dies In Fiery Smash Up*

11. *Man Dies From Multiple Stab Wounds After Fight With Alabama Man*

12. *Soldier Dies In Brave But Unnecessary Action*

13. *Native Americans Drown At River Crossing*

14. *Man Shot In Argument Over Dice Game* ✓

15. *Switchblade Serial Killer Strikes Again, Louie Miller Found Stabbed To Death*

16. *Flight #1203 Reported Missing*

17. *Unexpected Bend In Road Leads To Drag Race Tragedy*

18. *Cowboy Slain By Vigilantes While Returning To Scene Of The Crime*

19. *Two Men Rescued From Mine Cave In, One Missing, Cannibalism Feared*

20. *Biker Beau Crashes After Break-up*

(Answer key on page 85)

GRAMMAR—*Grammatically incorrect titles*

The titles of many Top 40 songs use improper English. For example, Helen Reddy's "Ain't No Way To Treat A Lady" is grammatically incorrect. The correct grammatical rephrasing would be:

"Your Behavior Toward Women Is Unacceptable."

Name the actual, grammatically incorrect Top 40 song titles for each of the reworded versions below.

One point for each correct song title.

1. "He's Easy To Lift Because Of Our Fraternal Relationship"

2. "(I'm Unable To Obtain) Contentment" ✓

3. "No Large Hill Is Too Steep" ✓

4. "I Possess Cadence"

5. "I'm Not Above Pleading With You" ✓

6.   "There Is No Female (Comparable To Mine)"

7.   "In What Direction Are You Headed, William?"

8.   "66% Is Pretty Good"

9.   "I Have No Interest In It"

10.   "Refrain From Directing Derogatory Comments At My Beloved"

11.   "Nothing Compares To Genuineness"

12.   "Has Calmness Eluded You In Your Lifetime?"

13.   "Boogie Oogie Oogie-ing Isn't Your Mother's Thing"

14.   "I'm Not The One, Sweetheart"

15.   "Things Don't Occur Without Difficulty"

16.   "It's Understood By Me (Your Affection For Me Is Gone)"

17.   "It's Cloudy (Forever)"

18.   "I Am Without A Residence"

19.   "Emancipation Is Correct For The Citizens"

20.   "Not A Thing Has Been Received By Us So Far"

(Answer key on page 87)

PUBLIC SPEAKING—*Spoken lyrics*

Provide the song title in which you'd hear following spoken lyrics.

One point for each correct song title.

---

1. "Second verse, same as the first."

2. "I won't be able to see you anymore because of my obligations and the ties that you have."

3. "You broke my heart, cause I couldn't dance, you didn't even want me around."

4. "We don't only sing but we dance just as good as we walk."

5. "You stripped me of my dreams, you gave me faith, then took my hope. Look at me now."

6. "The radio is blasting, someone's knocking at the door, I'm lookin' at my girlfriend, she's passed out on the floor."

7. "How do you call your lover boy?" "Come here, lover boy."

8.   "On board were the twelve: the poet, the physician, the farmer, the scientist, the magician, and the other so-called gods of our legends."

9.   "We laugh, tell a few jokes, but it still doesn't ease my pain."

10.   "Who's that flying up there? Is it a bird? (No!) Is it a plane? (No!)"

11.   "OK, so you're heartbroken. You sit around moping, cryin' and cryin'."

12.   "You know, every now and then I think you like to hear something from us nice and easy."

13.   "Honey, you lied when you said you loved me, and I had no cause to doubt you."

14.   "The pitcher glances over, winds up, and it's bunted, bunted down the third base line."

15.   "This is the police. Give yourself up."

16.   "And he'd be tall and handsome, rich and strong."

17.   "I ain't got nooooo money, honey."

18.   "Big boys don't cry. Big boys don't cry."

19.   "I dreamed I was in a Hollywood movie and that I was the star of the movie. This really blew my mind."

20.   "He went away and you hung around and bothered me every night, and when I wouldn't go out with you, you said things that weren't very nice."

(Answer key on page 89)

SPELLING—*Spelled out lyrics; artist name spelling bee*

> **Part 1: Name the Top 40 song in which the listed artists spell out a word in the lyrics.**
>
> **One point for each correct song title.**

1. Aretha Franklin

2. The Shadows of Knight

3. The Shangri-Las

4. The Kinks

5. The Bay City Rollers

6. Herman's Hermits

7. Connie Francis

8. The Echoes

9. Bobby Vinton

10. Carla Thomas

Part 2: *Correctly spell* the name of the artists who charted with the following Top 40 hits.

One point for each correctly spelled artist.

11. "A Whiter Shade Of Pale" and "Homburg"

12. "Sweet Home Alabama" and "Free Bird"

13. "You're No Good" and "Long Long Time"

14. "Red Rubber Ball" and "Turn Down Day"

15. "Born To Run" and "Hungry Heart"

16. "Beechwood 4-5679" and "Don't Mess With Bill"

17. "Walk Away Renee" and "Pretty Ballerina"

18. "More Today Than Yesterday"

19. "Everybody's Talkin'" and "Me and My Arrow"

20. "Release Me (And Let Me Love Again)" and "After The Lovin'"

(Answer key on page 91)

DICTIONARY SKILLS—Scrambled lyrics

> Lexicographer P. Odie Button was instructed to alphabetize 1967 song titles, but instead alphabetized their first lines! For example, his entry for A Whiter Shade of Pale was:
> "fandango light skipped the we"
> He placed each word of the song's first line ("We skipped the light fandango") in alphabetical order!
>
> Unscramble the following first lines of these 1967 tunes to name the song.
> One point for each correct song title.

1. cool evening everything getting groovy in is kind of of the the when

2. behave children say that's they together we're what when

3. and bite feeling fish low now the when won't you're

4. and are biting days gone nails of schoolgirl tales telling those

5. be it know that untrue would you

6. all and are baby I it know need the woman you you

7. be found is lies the to truth when

8.   bad everybody feels me Monday morning nag seems so to

9.   a a blue day in park sky sunshine take the to walk what

10.   be come fun gee here I not or ready such that to used

11.   and as baby black clean come door face is my night shining to

12.   feel I looking morning on out rain the to uninspired used /

13.   came days did go hey rain the we when where

14.   came from never say she she where would

15.   a dock fishin' in on she sits the the uh-huh water

16.   a deceived here's I know me now surprise you've

17.   a been for get I've long time to to trying you /

18.   all and come did of talk the things today we /

19.   don't if love me me tell why won't you you /

20.   a aeroplane an for gimme ticket //

(Answer key on page 93)

Test Two

Mathematics

"I say over and over and over again"

EXPONENTS—*Repetitive titles*

> Some song titles are exponential, consisting solely of the same word repeated two, three, or even more times, such as Ohio Express' "Yummy Yummy Yummy."
>
> Name the only Top 40 repetitively titled song by each of the following artists.
>
> One point for each correct song title.

1. The Mamas and The Papas

2. Tommy James and The Shondells

3. Gary Puckett and The Union Gap

4. Johnny Mathis

5. The Hollies

6. Neil Diamond

7. The Beau Brummels

8. The Castaways

9. Alive and Kicking

10.   The Playmates

11.   Cher

12.   The Dixie Cups

13.   Sopwith "Camel"

14.   Bobby Rydell

15.   The Kingsmen

16.   Major Lance

17.   Shirley and Company

18.   The New Christy Minstrels

19. and 20.

The Beach Boys had two Top 40 hits that were exponentially titled. For one point each, name both of these songs.

(Answer key on page 95)

STATISTICS—*Chart Position*

> **Of the following sets, choose the song which charted highest on the Billboard Top 40.**
>
> **One point for each correct answer.**

1. This Is It (Kenny Loggins)
   Are You Ready? (Pacific Gas and Electric)
   Yes, I'm Ready (Barbara Mason)

2. Hurt So Bad (Little Anthony and The Imperials)
   Hurts So Good (John Cougar)
   Love Is A Hurtin' Thing (Lou Rawls)

3. Here Comes My Baby (The Tremeloes)
   There Goes My Baby (The Drifters)
   Easy Come, Easy Go (Bobby Sherman)

4. Mercy (Ohio Express)
   Mercy, Mercy (Don Covay)
   Mercy, Mercy, Mercy (Buckinghams)

5.   Oh No (The Commodores)
      Oh Yeah (The Shadows of Knight)
      Maybe (The Chantels)

6.   White On White (Danny Williams)
      Black Is Black (Los Bravos)
      Touch Of Grey (Grateful Dead)

7.   Fa-Fa-Fa-Fa-Fa (Otis Redding)
      Um, Um, Um, Um, Um, Um (Major Lance)
      De Do Do Do, De Da Da Da (The Police)

8.   Happy Jack (The Who)
      Master Jack (Four Jacks and A Jill)
      Hit The Road Jack (Ray Charles)

9.   Little Bit O' Soul (The Music Explosion)
      Little Bit Of Soap (The Jarmels)
      Little Bit Of Heaven (Ronnie Dove)

10.   ABC (Jackson Five)
      1,2,3 (Len Barry)
      Do Re Mi (Lee Dorsey)

11.   Six O'Clock (The Lovin' Spoonful)
      Quarter To Three (Gary U.S. Bonds)
      Twelve Thirty (The Mamas and The Papas)

12.   Tuesday Afternoon (Moody Blues)
      Friday On My Mind (Easybeats)
      Come Saturday Morning (Sandpipers)

13.   Pink Cadillac (Natalie Cole)
      Hot Rod Lincoln (Commander Cody)
      Little Deuce Coupe (The Beach Boys)

14. My Last Date With You (Skeeter Davis)
Did It In A Minute (Hall and Oates)
You Can't Hurry Love (The Supremes)

15. Mr. Lee (The Bobbettes)
Mr. Bojangles (Nitty Gritty Dirt Band)
Mr. Big Stuff (Jean Knight)

16. Please Stay (The Drifters)
Go Now! (The Moody Blues)
Did You Ever Have To Make Up Your Mind? (The Lovin' Spoonful)

17. Oye Como Va (Santana)
El Condor Pasa (Simon and Garfunkel)
La Bamba (Ritchie Valens)

18. G.T.O. (Ronny and The Daytonas)
S.O.S. (Abba)
M.T.A. (The Kingston Trio)

19. Jesus Christ Superstar (Murray Head)
Hair (The Cowsills)
Day By Day (The Cast of Godspell)

20. So Long Baby (Del Shannon)
It's All Over Now (The Rolling Stones)
The End (Earl Grant)

(Answer key on page 97)

"Just the two of us, we can make it if we try"

SET THEORY—Artists with two #1 hits

> **The following artists attained the ultimate commercial success twice, with a set of #1 hits on the charts. Name both of their #1 hits.**
>
> **.5 point for each correct answer.**

1.   The Byrds

2.   Jim Croce

3.   Tommy James and The Shondells

4.   The Righteous Brothers

5.   Ricky Nelson

6.   America

7.   The Shirelles

8.   Petula Clark

9.   The Doors

10. Billy Preston

11. The Four Tops

12.   Queen

13.   The Association

14.   The Fifth Dimension

15.   The Doobie Brothers

16.   Frankie Avalon

17.   Grand Funk

18.   The Captain and Tennille

19.   Tommy Roe

20.   Glen Campbell

(Answer key on page 99)

"Say I am (what I am)"

ALGEBRA—*Parenthetical titles*

> **Fill in the missing variable to solve for the Top 40 parenthetical song title.**
>
> **One point for each correct answer.**

1. _____ (It's In His Kiss) ✓

2. _____ (With Glasses)

3. _____ (You're a Fine Girl) ✓

4. _____ (Day-O)

5. _____ (Forever Afternoon)

6. _____ (Falettinme Be Mice Elf Agin) ✓

7. _____ (Don't Worry 'Bout Me)

8. _____ (And You Alone)

9. _____ (Quinn The Eskimo)

10. _____ (That's What I Want) ✓

11. Hello Muddah Hello Faddah (_____) ✓

12. Any Day Now (_____) ✓

13. Da Doo Ron Ron (_____) ✎

14. In The Year 2525 (_____)

15. Mercy Mercy Me (_____)

16. Remember (_____)

17. Life Is A Rock (_____)

18. Society's Child (_____)

19. 634-5789 (_____) ✎

20. Double Shot (_____)

(Answer key on page 101)

"Now gimme money, that's what I want"

FINANCE—*Monetary lyrics*

> **Fill in the blank with the correct amount of money mentioned in the following lyrics.**
>
> **One point for each correct answer.**

1. From The Turtles' "Happy Together":
    "If I should call you up, invest a _____."

2. From Joni Mitchell's "Big Yellow Taxi":
    "They took all the trees, and put 'em in a tree museum, and they charged all the people _____ just to see 'em."

3. From The Rolling Stones' "19th Nervous Breakdown":
    "Your mother who neglected you owes a _____ tax."

4. From Billy J. Kramer with The Dakotas' "Little Children":
    "Little children, you better not tell what you see, and if you're good I'll give you candy and _____."

5. From Roger Miller's "Dang Me":
    "Spent the groceries and half the rent, like _____."

6. From Dr. Hook and the Medicine Show's "Sylvia's Mother":
"And the operator says _____ more for the next three minutes."

7. From The Kingston Trio's "MTA":
"When he got there the conductor told him 'one more _____,' Charlie couldn't get off of that train."

8. From Ray Peterson's "Tell Laura I Love Her":
"He saw a sign for a stock car race, _____ prize, it read."

9. From Arlo Guthrie's "Alice's Restaurant":
"And we was fined _____ and had to pick up the garbage in the snow."

10. From Glen Campbell's "Rhinestone Cowboy":
"And I dream of the things I'll do, with a subway token and _____ tucked inside my shoe."

11. From The Five Americans' "Western Union":
"_____ a word to read, a telegram I didn't need."

12. From Peter, Paul and Mary's "500 Miles":
"Not a shirt on my back not _____ to my name, Lord I can't go a-home this-a way."

13. From Dionne Warwick's "Do You Know The Way To San Jose?":
"Put _____ down and buy a car."

14. From Roger Miller's "King of the Road":
"Trailer for sale or rent, rooms to let _____."

15. and 16.
From Harry Chapin's "Taxi":
"And she handed me a _____ for a _____ fare, she said, 'Harry, keep the change.'"

17. and 18.

> From Creedence Clearwater Revival's "Down on the Corner":
> "You don't need a _____ just to hang around,
> but if you've got a _____ won't you lay your
> money down?"

19. and 20.

> From Bob Dylan's "Subterranean Homesick Blues":
> "The man in the coonskin cap in the big pen wants
> _____ bills, you only got _____."

(Answer key on page 103)

ADDITION—*Singers and their back-up groups*

> **Many bands identify themselves by adding the name of their lead singer to the name given to the back-up singers/musicians.**
>
> **Part one: Name the groups associated with the following lead singers.**
>
> **One point for each correct answer.**

1. Gladys Knight + ?
2. J. Frank Wilson + ?
3. Jr. Walker + ?
4. Gene Vincent + ?
5. Sam The Sham + ?
6. Mitch Ryder + ?
7. Rick Nelson + ?
8. Wayne Fontana + ?

9.   Tommy James   +   ?

10. Gary Lewis   +   ?

Part two: Name the lead singers associated with the following groups.

One point for each correct answer.

---

11. ?   +   His Dominoes

12. ?   +   The Union Gap

13. ?   +   The Silver Bullet Band

14. ?   +   The Fireballs

15. ?   +   The Heywoods

16. ?   +   The Midnighters

17. ?   +   Dawn

18. ?   +   Brasil '66

19. ?   +   His Ray Men

20. ?   +   The Teenagers

(Answer key on page 105)

Test Three

Social Studies

U.S. GEOGRAPHY—
American cities in lyrics

> **Answer with the U.S. city mentioned in the songs below.**
>
> **One point for each correct answer.**

1. According to The Standells in "Dirty Water," what U.S. city do they call home?

2. In what U.S. city are The Eagles standing on a corner in "Take It Easy"?

3. In the Dr. Hook song "Sylvia's Mother," where does Sylvia's intended husband live?

4. What city is featured with lunar prominence in the theme song from the movie *Arthur*?

5. What U.S. city is home to Archie Bell and The Drells in "Tighten Up"? ✓

6. According to Jim Croce, in what city did "Bad, Bad, Leroy Brown" live? ✓

35

7.   According to Georgie Fame's "The Ballad of Bonnie and Clyde," out of what town did the couple high-tail, following a store robbery there one lazy afternoon?

8.   According to Stevie Wonder in "I Was Made To Love Her," where was he born? ✓

9.   In what city is "a poor little baby child born" in Elvis Presley's "In The Ghetto"?

10.   According to Ike and Tina Turner in "Proud Mary," in what city did they "clean a lot of plates"?

11.   In Lou Reed's "Walk On The Wild Side," from what city did Holly come?

12.   Where did Simon and Garfunkel board a Greyhound Bus in "America"?

13.   In "Brown Sugar," where did The Rolling Stones meet a "gin soaked bar room queen"?

14.   According to O.C. Smith in "Little Green Apples," in what city doesn't it rain in the summertime? ✓

15.   What U.S. city "proved to be too much for the man" in Gladys Knight and The Pips' "Midnight Train To Georgia"? ✓

16.   According to Johnny Horton, from what U.S. city did Big Sam depart to go "North To Alaska"?

17.   To what city are The Allman Brothers headed this morning in "Ramblin' Man"?

18., 19., and 20.
        For one point each, identify the three Top 40 song titles by Glen Campbell that contain the names of U.S. cities.

(Answer key on page 107)

BRITISH HISTORY—Last lines of Beatles songs

> **The British Invasion began with The Beatles, whose impact on music was historic. Identify the Beatles song titles by their last lines.**
>
> **One point for each correct song title.**

1. "You're gonna say you love me too, you love me too."

2. "My baby don't care." ✓

3. "All the lonely people, where do they all belong?"

4. "Making all his nowhere plans for nobody."

5. "And she keeps calling me back again."

6. "With a love like that you know you should be glad, yeah yeah yeah, yeah yeah yeah, yeah yeah yeah yeah." ✓

7. "The way things are going, they're going to crucify me."

8. "Say the words you long to hear, I'm in love with you, oo-oo-ooh, oo-oo-ooh."

9. "I don't want to leave her now, you know I believe and how."

10.   "Baby take a chance with me."

11.   "Tuesday on the phone to me, oh yeah."

12.   "1-2-3-4-5-6-7, all good children go to heaven." ✓

13.   "All you gotta do is call and I'll be there." ✓

14.   "Wonder how you manage to feed the rest."

15.   "And the eyes in his head see the world spinning round."

16.   "Yes it's so hard loving you, loving you."

17.   "You know I feel all right."

18.   "Dying to take you away, take you today."

19.   "You were only waiting for this moment to arrive."

20   "The love you take is equal to the love you make."

(Answer key on page 109)

"Say it loud, I'm black and I'm proud"

BLACK HISTORY—*Motown*

Fill in the blanks, one for each word, with the Top 40 Motown song title that completes the lyrics. Titles are presented alphabetically.

One point for each correct answer.

---

1. *Beginning with the letter A:*
   "_ _ _, easy as one, two three, oh simple as do re mi."

2. *Beginning with the letter B:*
   "_____, people are searchin' for the kind of love that we possess."

3. *Beginning with the letter C:*
   "Cause I've found me somebody new, ____ ___ ___ _____
   _____."

4. *Beginning with the letter D:*
   "Hear what I say, girls keep away, ____ ____ ____ ____."

5. *Beginning with the letter E:*
   "_____ _____ ___ _____, to you I'm a toy and you're the boy who has to say when I should play.

39

✓ 6. *Beginning with the letter F:*
"___ ____ __ __ ____, I have someone who needs me, someone I've needed so long."

✓ 7. *Beginning with the letter G:*
"And don't be shocked if you see your favorite star-a _____ __ _ __ __."

✓ 8. *Beginning with the letter H:*
"Could it be a devil in me or is this the way it's supposed to be? It's like a ____ ____."

✓ 9. *Beginning with the letter I:*
"_ _____ __ _____ ___ _____, and I'm just about to lose my mind, honey honey."

✓ 10. *Beginning with the letter J:*
"Out of all the fellows in the world she belongs to me, but it was ____ __ _____."

✓ 11. *Beginning with the letter K:*
"I'll be the red ball express of lovin', I'll ____ __ _____."

✓ 12. *Beginning with the letter L:*
"The _____ ___ ____ may be your own, darlin' look both ways before you cross me."

✓ 13. *Beginning with the letter M:*
"Nothing you could say could tear me away from __ ___."

✓ 14. *Beginning with the letter N:*
"Just keeps me, keeps me crying myself to sleep, he brings _____ ___ _____."

✓ 15. *Beginning with the letter O:*
"And in the game I lost you, what a price to pay, I'm crying, ___ ____ ___."

16. *Beginning with the letter P:*
    "You shake up the whole town, and that's why you are my
    _____ __ __."

17. *Beginning with the letter Q:*
    "Your love is like _____, pulling me deeper and deeper
    in love with you."

18. *Beginning with the letter R:*
    "I'm a ____ _____ baby, can't stay in one place too long."

19. *Beginning with the letter S:*
    "_____ __ honey, good times never felt so good."

20. *Beginning with the letter T:*
    "____ __ _____ __ ____ been broke a thousand times."

(Answer key on page 111)

"God only knows what I'd be without you"

RELIGION—*Teen idols*

Identify the teenage heart-throbs from the information below.
One point for each correct answer.

1.   He penned the theme song for *The Tonight Show*.

2.   He dated actress Victoria Principal and was thought to have beaten his drug addiction when he died of a viral heart inflammation at age 30.

3.   American fans knew him first as Dr. Noah Drake on *General Hospital*.

4.   Mr. Ridarelli appeared as Hugo Peabody in the film *Bye Bye Birdie*.

5.   He was best known as "Moondoggie" in the *Gidget* movie series.

6.   He was a *Shindig!* regular and starred in *Here Come The Brides*.

7.   His autobiography, *Come On, Get Happy*, was published in 1994.

8.   This enigmatic talent and self-proclaimed "King of Pop" successfully bid against Paul McCartney and Yoko Ono for ownership of 250 Lennon/McCartney songs.

9.   Walden Robert Cassotto worked on Robert Kennedy's presidential campaign.

10. After his popularity waned, he and his sister did commercials for Hawaiian Punch.

11. From 1975 to 1978, he hosted a musical variety series; his later hits became polka classics.

12. His back-up group was named for the Bronx avenue where their street corner singing received raves.

13. Mr. Forte starred with John Wayne in the film *North To Alaska*.

14. A malfunctioning gas heater, not freebasing, caused the New Year's eve plane crash that took his life.

15. He and Shelley Fabares played the teenage children on *The Donna Reed Show*.

16. Founder of the group Humble Pie, he played Billy Shears in the film *Sgt. Pepper's Lonely Hearts Club Band*.

17. Mr. Velline got his break filling in for Buddy Holly the day after Holly's plane crash.

18. The most enduring rock and roll icon of all time, his addiction to prescription drugs led to his deadly heart attack at age 42.

19. Shirley Jones' son, he starred as Joe Hardy on the TV show *The Hardy Boys*.

20. He appeared opposite Annette Funicello in *Beach Blanket Bingo*.

(Answer key on page 113)

PSYCHOLOGY—*Bad #1 hits of the '70s*

Psychologists have yet to explain the success of several chart-toppers from the early to mid -1970s. From the lyric snippets below, name these #1 hits which, despite their popularity, many consider horrendous.

One point for each correct song title.

1. "No one else can make me feel the colors that you bring. Stay with me while we grow old and we will live each day in springtime."

2. "I'm afraid that I'm not sure of a love there is no cure for."

3. "Someone else will come along, and sock it to ya again."

4. "Talk about your childhood wishes, you can even eat the dishes."

5. "There was a funky China man, from a funky China town."

6. "When the sun's coming up I got cakes on the griddle."

7. "Rubbin' sticks and stones together makes the sparks ignite."

8. "So many days, I sit by my window, waiting for someone, to sing me a song."

9.   "To take you to his mansion in the sky."

10.   "They'd sent some reinforcements, from the Illinois National Guard."

11.   "Jesus loves the little children, all the children of the world."

12.   "I'm really still in prison and my love she holds the key."

13.   "You could have swept it from your life but you didn't do it."

14.   "Tears are in my eyes, and nothing is rhyming."

15.   "Cause I'll just use you then I'll set you free."

16.   "Once I was swimming 'cross Turtle Creek, man those snappers all around my feet."

17.   "So they sprinkled moon dust in your hair of gold and starlight in your eyes of blue."

18.   "You make me sing like a guitar hummin'."

19.   "Think of me babe whenever some sweet talkin' girl comes along."

20.   "Learned of love and ABC's, skinned our hearts and skinned our knees."

(Answer key on page 115)

COUNTERCULTURE—*Peace and protest songs*

> **Name the songs of peace and protest in which you'd hear the following lyrics.**
>
> **One point for each correct answer.**

1. "The eastern world, it is explodin', violence flarin', bullets loadin'."

2. "Gotta get down to it, soldiers are gunning us down, should have been done long ago."

3. "We are but a moment's sunlight, fading in the grass."

4. "Why must we go on hating, why can't we live in bliss?"

5. "(Generals order their soldiers to kill) and to gather it all in a bunch of heather (and to fight for a cause they've long ago forgotten)."

6. "Yesterday my friends were marching out to war, well listen now we ain't a-marchin' anymore."

7. "A time for love, a time for hate, a time for peace, I swear it's not too late."

8. "Do you ask why I'm sighing my son? You shall inherit what mankind has done."

/ 9. "He freed a lot of people but seems the good they die young."

10. "Some folks inherit star spangled eyes, ooh they send you down to war, lord."

11. "Cannon fire lingers in my mind, I'm so glad that I'm still alive."

12. "How many deaths will it take till he knows that too many people have died?"

/ 13. "Father father, there's no need to escalate, war is not the answer."

14. "Come Senators, Congressmen, please heed the call, don't stand in the doorway, don't block up the hall."

/ 15. "An eye for an eye, a tooth for a tooth, vote for me and I'll set you free."

16. "Listen please listen, that's the way it should be, peace in the valley."

17. "We all had caught the same disease and we all sang songs of peace."

18. "He blesses the boys as they stand in line, the smell of gun grease and the bayonets they shine."

19. "When you talk about destruction, don't you know that you can count me out."

20. "There's a man with a gun over there telling me I got to beware."

(Answer key on page 117)

Test Four

Science

ZOOLOGY—Animals in song titles

> **Name the only Top 40 song title by each of the following artists that mentions a type of animal.**
>
> **One point for each correct answer.**

1. Carly Simon and James Taylor
2. Lobo
3. Major Lance
4. The Lovin' Spoonful
5. Jefferson Airplane
6. Harry Chapin
7. The Rolling Stones
8. Bobby Day
9. The Steve Miller Band
10. The Captain and Tennille
11. Tom Jones
12. Lynyrd Sknyrd

13.   The Ohio Players

14.   George Harrison

15.   Al Stewart

16.   Ted Nugent

17.   America

18.   Bob Lind

19. and 20.

Elton John had two Top 40 hits with animals in the titles. For one point each, name both of these songs.

(Answer key on page 119)

PRE-MED—*Musical maladies*

> **Name the song that best fits the named artists' medical conditions.**
>
> **One point for each correct answer.**

1. The doctor suggested Benadryl for the Coasters' bad case of: ___?___.

2. "Take two aspirin and call me in the morning," was the doctor's advice regarding Peggy Lee's: ___?___.

3. "I've seen bloating like this thousands of times," said the gastroenterologist to Mason Williams. "You have: ___?___."

4. Realizing that she was behind in her inoculations, Pat Benatar said to the doctor: "___?___."

5. The neurologist feared a mild stroke when The Searchers complained of: ___?___.

6. "I think I know what is causing your allergies," said the doctor to the group Kansas. "It's: ___?___."

7. The doctor confirmed the diagnosis of black lung disease when he learned that Lee Dorsey had spent years: ___?___.

8. What did the doctor tell the nurses to do to help the bedridden Byrds avoid bedsores? ___?___

9. The surgical team's operation was a total success! Former Siamese Twin Lou Christie will no longer have to sing: ___?___.

10. Speaking of Siamese, what illness do you suppose Ted Nugent has? ___?___

11. The psychiatrists are admitting The Rolling Stones yet again to the Psychiatric Ward because it's their: ___?___.

12. Manfred Mann went to the ophthalmologist because he was: ___?___.

13. The proctologist advised The Dovells, "Yes, hemorrhoids are serious when: ___?___."

14. The obstetrician received a call from Paul Anka, who said, "It's time! She's: ___?___."

15. Mrs. Santo and Mrs. Johnny called the doctor because of their husbands' nightly: ___?___.

16. The doctor suspected the D.T.s when the Guess Who came to the office: ___?___.

17. "Doctor," said The Serendipity Singers, "Do you think my hearing loss could be explained by the: ___?___?"

18. An inner ear infection could explain why Tommy Roe feels so: ___?___.

19. Johnny Rivers' two-fold illness was diagnosed as: ___?___.

20. Triple bypass surgery was necessary following Olivia Newton-John's: ___?___.

(Answer key on page 121)

"Time has come today"

EVOLUTION—*Times in lyrics and titles*

> **Evolution is the study of change over time, a theme found in many songs.**
>
> **Part 1: Name the times mentioned in the following songs.**
>
> **One point for each correct answer.**

1. At what hour do Bill Haley and His Comets yell for more in "Rock Around The Clock"?

2. In "Expressway To Your Heart," what time is it "much too crowded"?

3. In "Chantilly Lace," what time is the Big Bopper's date?

4. What time do the Monkees set their alarm in "Daydream Believer"?

5. In The Beatles' "She's Leaving Home," at what time does she close her bedroom door?

6. Until what time did the Four Freshmen dance at their "Graduation Day" Prom?

7.   What time does Lee Dorsey get up to begin his day "Working In The Coal Mine"?

8.   At what time do the Everly Brothers "Wake Up Little Susie"?

9.   What time does the regular crowd shuffle in to see Billy Joel, "The Piano Man"?

10.   In Chuck Berry's "Reeling And Rocking," when did he not know if he was dead or alive?

Part 2: Identify the "Time" song titles from the lyrics.

One point for each correct answer.

---

11.   "Tumble out of bed and stumble to the kitchen, pour myself a cup of ambition."

12.   "Tradin' my time for the pay I get, livin' on money that I ain't made yet."

13.   "There's another before me, you'll never be mine, I'm wasting my time."

14.   "Everybody was as happy as they could be 'cause they were swingin' with Daddy G."

15.   "I'm gonna wait till the stars come out and see that twinkle in your eyes."

16.   "Staring blindly into space, getting up to splash my face."

17.   "And I think we can make it, one more time, if we try."

18.   "I can no longer keep my blinds drawn, and I can't keep myself from talking."

19. "I wish my head had been working right, we'd have gone for coffee and talked all night."

20. "Shadows paintin' our faces, traces of romance in our heads."

(Answer key on page 123)

CHEMISTRY—*Titles ending with "love"*

Name the only Top 40 song title by each of the following artists that ends with the word *"love"*

One point for each correct song title.

1. Lulu

2. The Dixie Cups

3. The Steve Miller Band

4. David Bowie

5. Jefferson Airplane

6. The Eagles

7. The Association

8. Cream

9. The Four Tops /

10. David Ruffin /

11. The Crystals

12. Led Zeppelin /

13.   Jackie DeShannon

14.   Jackson Browne

15.   Dion and The Belmonts

16.   Peter and Gordon

17.   The Yardbirds

18.   The Everly Brothers

19. and 20.

The Mamas and The Papas hit the Top 40 charts twice with song titles that ended with the word "*love*." For one point each, name both songs.

(Answer key on page 125)

HUMAN PHYSIOLOGY—
Body parts in titles

> **Name the only Top 40 song title by each of the following artists that mentions a part of the body.**
>
> **One point for each correct answer.**

1. The Platters /

2. Fleetwood Mac

3. John Denver

4. Roberta Flack /

5. Jackson Browne

6. The Pointer Sisters

7. The Doobie Brothers

8. Joe Tex /

9. Slim Harpo /

10. Electric Light Orchestra

11.   Crosby, Stills and Nash

12.   Johnny Crawford

13.   James Taylor

14.   Little Anthony and The Imperials

15.   The Grassroots

16.   Lou Christie

17.   The Everly Brothers

18.   Foreigner

19. and 20.

   ZZ Top had two Top 40 hits with body parts in the titles. For one point each, name both songs.

   (Answer key on page 127)

THE SCIENTIFIC METHOD—
Titles posed as questions

> **Scientists ask hypothetical questions as they develop their theories. Given the following cryptic responses, determine the Top 40 song titles, all in question format, which prompted these answers.**
>
> **One point for each correct song title.**

1. Yes. Going north from L.A., go through Salinas. It's just northeast of Santa Cruz.

2. Gee, no. Since no one here wears a watch, we just estimate the hour.

3. Of course I will darling. Just as I did yesterday, and I do today.

4. Here they are! I cut them from the garden and put them into vases for a dining room centerpiece.

5. Yes I do. The Twist, The Hustle or The Macarena?

6. Oh, she definitely is! She has his class ring on a chain and his letter sweater.

7.   Well, the best way is through surgery. Call your cardiologist for an appointment.

8.   Sure you do. It's guaranteed by the constitution.

9.   No, it's just as tasty in the morning. Hard as a rock, maybe, but still yummy.

10.   Maybe an Indian will. I know they have dances that can start it.

11.   No, as a matter of fact, the thought of you naked makes me want to vomit.

12.   It's next to the elementary school. Look, there's the slide, the swings and the sandbox.

13.   No! Don't tell me! I'm such a gossip, I couldn't possibly keep it to myself!

14.   Yep, she's there in the shade with my daddy.

15.   Well, of course. What else would a hula hoop do?

16.   Because geniuses are too smart to leave themselves emotionally exposed.

17.   Yes, it *would* be lovely!

18.   Yes! No! Gee, I can't decide!

19.   No, I'm totally apathetic.

20.   Yep, that's all. Life is nothing more, nothing less.

(Answer key on page 129)

Test Five

The Arts

Fine Arts—Classic rock albums

> **The albums listed below are classics, representing the finest in rock and roll.**
>
> **Name the artists associated with these classic album titles.**
>
> **One point for each correct answer.**

1. "Disraeli Gears"

2. "Cheap Thrills"

3. "52nd Street"

4. "The Dark Side Of The Moon" /

5. "If You Can Believe Your Eyes and Ears"

6. "American Beauty"

7. "Tea For The Tillerman"

8. "Pet Sounds"

9. "Sticky Fingers"

10. "Rumours"

11 "Days Of Future Passed"

12.   "Greetings From Asbury Park, N.J."

13.   "Highway 61 Revisited"

14.   "Whipped Cream (and Other Delights)"

15.   "Tumbleweed Connection"

16.   "Court and Spark"

17.   "Innervisions"/

18.   "Four Way Street"

19.   "461 Ocean Boulevard"

20.   "Fragile"

(Answer key on page 131)

"I write the songs that make the whole world sing"

AUTHORS—*Singer-Songwriters*

Many artists first made their mark as songwriters. Name the Top 40 artists who are credited with writing or co-writing each of the following sets of Top 40 songs for other performers.

One point for each correct artist.

1. "Go Away Little Girl" (Steve Lawrence)
   "Will You Love Me Tomorrow" (The Shirelles)
   "One Fine Day" (The Chiffons)

2. "Hello Mary Lou" (Rick Nelson)
   "He's A Rebel" (The Crystals)
   "Rubber Ball" (Bobby Vee)

3. "Wedding Bell Blues" (The Fifth Dimension)
   "Stoney End" (Barbra Streisand)
   "And When I Die" (Blood, Sweat and Tears)

4. "Pretty Paper" (Roy Orbison)
   "Hello Walls" (Faron Young)
   "Crazy" (Patsy Cline)

5.   "Love Will Keep Us Together" (The Captain and Tennille)
     "I Waited Too Long" (LaVerne Baker)
     "Solitaire" (The Carpenters)

6.   "Dum Dum" (Brenda Lee)
     "Bette Davis Eyes" (Kim Carnes)
     "When You Walk In The Room" (The Searchers)

7.   "Don't Mess With Bill" (The Marvelettes)
     "The Way You Do The Things You Do" (The Temptations)
     "My Guy" (Mary Wells)

8.   "Sunday and Me" (Jay and The Americans)
     "I'm A Believer" (The Monkees)
     "Sunflower" (Glen Campbell)

9.   "If Not For You" (Olivia Newton-John)
     "The Mighty Quinn" (Manfred Mann)
     "All I Really Want To Do" (Cher)

10. "Down In The Boondocks" (Billy Joe Royal)
     "Hush" (Deep Purple)
     "I Never Promised You A Rose Garden" (Lynn Anderson)

11. "Teddy" (Connie Francis)
     "She's A Lady" (Tom Jones)
     "My Way" (Frank Sinatra)

12. "Then You Can Tell Me Goodbye" (The Casinos)
     "Indian Reservation" (The Raiders)
     "Norman" (Sue Thompson)

13. "I Can't Turn You Loose" (Chambers Brothers)
     "Sweet Soul Music" (Arthur Conley)
     "Respect" (Aretha Franklin)

14. "Goodbye" (Mary Hopkin)
    "Come and Get It" (Badfinger)
    "Woman" (Peter and Gordon)

15. "Everybody Loves A Clown" (Gary Lewis and The Playboys)
    "This Masquerade" (George Benson)
    "Superstar" (The Carpenters)

16. "In The Ghetto" (Elvis Presley)
    "I Believe In Music" (Gallery)
    "Watching Scotty Grow" (Bobby Goldsboro)

17. "Help Me Make It Through The Night" (Gladys Knight and The Pips)
    "Me and Bobby McGee" (Janis Joplin)
    "For The Good Times" (Ray Price)

18. "Because The Night" (Patti Smith Group)
    "Fire" (The Pointer Sisters)
    "Pink Cadillac" (Natalie Cole)

19. "Soul Man" (Sam and Dave)
    "B-A-B-Y" (Carla Thomas)
    "Deja Vu" (Dionne Warwick)

20. "Nobody But Me" (Human Beinz)
    "Respectable" (The Outsiders)
    "Shout" (Joey Dee and The Starlighters)

(Answer key on page 133)

DANCE—Dance songs

> **Match the Top 40 dance songs on the left with their associated artists on the right.**
>
> **One point for each correct answer.**

1.	Wah-Wahtusi	A.	Rufus Thomas
2.	The Peppermint Twist	B.	The Larks
3.	The Jerk	C.	Dee Dee Sharp
4.	C'mon and Swim	D.	The Diamonds
5.	Do The Freddie	E.	The Dovells
6.	The Bristol Stomp	F.	Bent Fabric and His Piano
7.	Mashed Potato Time	G.	Fantastic Johnny C
8.	Boogaloo Down Broadway	H.	Bobby "Boris" Pickett
9.	The Hustle	I.	Joey Dee and The Starlighters
10.	The Alley Cat	J.	Chubby Checker

11.	Shimmy Shimmy Ko-Ko-Bop	K.	The Orlons
12.	Monkey Time	L.	Bobby Vinton
13.	(Do The) Funky Chicken	M.	Van McCoy
14.	The Cha-Cha-Cha	N.	Bobby Freeman
15.	Pony Time	O.	Bobby Rydell
16.	The Monster Mash	P.	Little Anthony and The Imperials
17.	Beer Barrel Polka	Q.	Freddie and The Dreamers
18.	The Stroll	R.	Major Lance

19. and 20.

Two artists hit #1 on the Billboard charts with the dance song "The Loco-Motion." For one point each, name both artists.

(Answer key on page 135)

THE GRAND MASTERS—
Artists' nicknames

> **Identify the music pioneers, all inductees of The Rock and Roll Hall of Fame, associated with the following nicknames.**
>
> **One point for each correct answer.**

1. The Hardest Working Man In Show Business ✓

2. The Man In Black

3. The Lizard King

4. Slowhand

5. Mr. Excitement

6. Satchmo ✓

7. Blue

8. The Queen of Soul ✓

9. Pearl

10. The Ice Man ✓

11.   The Killer

12.   The Boss ✓

13.   The King

14.   The Big O

15.   The Genius

16.   Mr. Personality ✓

17.   Wicked ✓

18.   The Gloved One ✓

19.   Mr. Soul

20.   The Fat Man

(Answer key on page 137)

FILM—Artists and songs featured in movies

Part 1: Many movies are about or feature Top 40 artists. Name the singer or group featured prominently in each of the following films.

One point for each correct answer.

---

1. *The Song Remains The Same*

2. *Don't Look Back*

3. *The Man Who Fell To Earth*

4. *Gimme Shelter*

5. *Hold On*

6. *Having A Wild Weekend*

7. *Head*

8. *Can't Stop The Music*

9. *The Kids Are Alright*

10. *The Last Waltz*

Part 2: Several songs that became hit records were introduced in movies. Name the films in which the following Top 40 hits were featured.

One point for each correct movie title.

11.   "Raindrops Keep Falling On My Head" by B. J. Thomas

12.   "The Morning After" by Maureen McGovern

13.   "Come Saturday Morning" by The Sandpipers

14.   "Everybody's Talking" by Nilsson

15.   "For All We Know" by The Carpenters

16.   "Mrs. Robinson" by Simon and Garfunkel

17.   "I'm Easy" by Keith Carradine

18.   "How Deep Is Your Love" by The Bee Gees

19.   "Hopelessly Devoted to You" by Olivia Newton-John

20.   "Last Dance" by Donna Summer

(Answer key on page 139)

*"Laugh laugh, I thought I'd die,
it seemed so funny to me"*

COMEDY—*Novelty songs*

> **Name the Top 40 novelty songs containing the following lyrics.**
>
> **One point for each correct song title.**

1. "They got little cars that go beep-beep-beep."

2. "You remember Jeffrey Hardy, they're about to organize a searching party."

3. "You left me anyhow and then the days got worse and worse."

4. "My fist got hard and my wits got keen."

5. "And then he swung from the tree and he lit on the ground."

6. "Got a condo made of stone-a."

7. "Gotta find a woman! Gotta find a woman!"

8. "Right into the path of a runaway garbage truck."

9. "Look at 'em out there, runnin' around like a bunch of wild injuns."

10. "Jane gets right and the monkey gets tight."

11.   "The coffin baggers were about to arrive with their vocal group."

12.   "Shoot the juice to me, Bruce."

13.   "There was the same old shoot 'em up and the same old rodeo."

14.   "You could hear him swearin' 'ach du lieber!'"

15.   "Tried to amend my carnivorous habits, made it nearly seventy days."

16.   "Even on the range he used two sets of dishes."

17.   "He shoulda looked left and he shoulda looked right."

18.   "He got a big ugly club, and a head full of hair."

19.   "Cab over four with a reefer on."

20.   "You're the ginchiest!"

(Answer key on page 141)

Answer Keys

Scoring: One point for each correct answer, unless noted otherwise.

Foreign Language

Answer Key

1. Tutti-Frutti (Little Richard)

2. I Want To Take You Higher (Sly and the Family Stone)

3. Good Morning Starshine (Oliver)

4. The Boxer (Simon and Garfunkel)

5. He's So Fine (The Chiffons)

6. Hooked On A Feeling (Blue Swede)

7. Lady Marmalade (LaBelle)

8. Bad Girls (Donna Summer)

9. Sea Cruise (Frankie Ford)

10. Rockin' Robin (Bobby Day)

11. Witch Doctor (David Seville)

12. The Name Game (Shirley Ellis)

13. Winchester Cathedral (New Vaudeville Band)

14. The Lion Sleeps Tonight (The Tokens)

15. Breaking Up Is Hard To Do (Neil Sedaka)

16. '65 Love Affair (Paul Davis)

17. Get A Job (The Silhouettes)

18. Blue Moon (The Marcels)

19. Sweet City Woman (The Stampeders)

20. Hurdy Gurdy Man (Donovan)

TOTAL SCORE ON FOREIGN LANGUAGE SUBTEST: _____

Enter on line (1) on page 143

Journalism

Answer Key

1. Teen Angel (Mark Dinning)

2. Delilah (Tom Jones)

3. Ode To Billie Joe (Bobbie Gentry) √

4. Wreck of the Edmund Fitzgerald (Gordon Lightfoot)

5. Ohio (Crosby, Stills, Nash and Young) √

6. Space Oddity (David Bowie)

7. Honey (Bobby Goldsboro)

8. Ballad of the Green Berets (S. Sgt. Barry Sadler)

9. Big Bad John (Jimmy Dean)

10. Tell Laura I Love Her (Ray Peterson)

11. You Don't Mess Around With Jim (Jim Croce)

12. Billy, Don't Be A Hero (Bo Donaldson and The Heywoods)

13. Running Bear (Johnny Preston)

14. Stagger Lee (Lloyd Price) √

15. Mack The Knife (Bobby Darin)

16. Ebony Eyes (Everly Brothers)

17.   Dead Man's Curve (Jan and Dean)

18.   El Paso (Marty Robbins)

19.   Timothy (The Buoys)

20.   Leader of the Pack (The Shangri-Las)

TOTAL SCORE ON JOURNALISM SUBTEST: _____
Enter on line (2) on page 143

Grammar

Answer Key

1. He Ain't Heavy, He's My Brother (The Hollies)

2. (I Can't Get No) Satisfaction (The Rolling Stones)

3. Ain't No Mountain High Enough (Diana Ross)

4. I Got Rhythm (The Happenings)

5. Ain't Too Proud To Beg (The Temptations)

6. Ain't No Woman (Like The One I Got) (The Four Tops)

7. Which Way You Goin' Billy? (The Poppy Family)

8. Two Out Of Three Ain't Bad (Meatloaf)

9. It Don't Matter To Me (Bread)

10. Don't Say Nothing Bad About My Baby (The Cookies)

11. Ain't Nothing Like The Real Thing (Marvin Gaye and Tammi Terrill)

12. Have You Never Been Mellow? (Olivia Newton-John)

13. Your Mama Don't Dance (Loggins and Messina)

14. It Ain't Me Babe (The Turtles)

15. It Don't Come Easy (Ringo Starr)

/ 16.   I Know (You Don't Love Me No More) (Barbara George)

17.   The Sun Ain't Gonna Shine (Anymore) (The Walker Brothers)

18.   Ain't Got No Home (Clarence "Frogman" Henry)

19.   People Got To Be Free (The Rascals)

20.   We Ain't Got Nothin' Yet (The Blues Magoos)

TOTAL SCORE ON GRAMMAR TEST: _____
Enter on line (3) on page 143

Public Speaking

Answer Key

1. I'm Henry VIII, I Am (Herman's Hermits)

2. Kiss and Say Goodbye (The Manhattans)

3. Do You Love Me? (The Contours)

4. Tighten Up (Archie Bell and The Drells)

5. Love Is Here and Now You're Gone (The Supremes)

6. Mama Told Me Not To Come (Three Dog Night)

7. Love Is Strange (Mickey and Sylvia)

8. Atlantis (Donovan)

9. Have You Seen Her? (The Chi-Lites)

10. Let's Twist Again (Chubby Checker)

11. Everybody Plays The Fool (The Main Ingredient)

12. Proud Mary (Ike and Tina Turner)

13. Are You Lonesome Tonight? (Elvis Presley)

14. Paradise By The Dashboard Light (Meatloaf)

15. Indiana Wants Me (R. Dean Taylor)

16. He's Sure The Boy I Love (The Crystals)

17.   Chantilly Lace (The Big Bopper)

18.   I'm Not In Love (10 cc)

19.   Spill The Wine (Eric Burdon and War)

20.   My Boyfriend's Back (The Angels)

TOTAL SCORE ON PUBLIC SPEAKING SUBTEST: _____

Enter on line (4) on page 143

Spelling

Answer Key

1.   Respect

2.   Gloria

3.   Give Him A Great Big Kiss

4.   Lola

5.   Saturday Night

6.   I'm Henry VIII, I Am

7.   V-A-C-A-T-I-O-N

8.   Baby Blue

9.   L-O-N-E-L-Y

10. B-A-B-Y

11. Procol Harum

12. Lynyrd Skynyrd

13. Linda Ronstadt

14. The Cyrkle

15. Bruce Springsteen

16. The Marvelettes

17.   The Left Banke

18.   Spiral Starecase

19.   Nilsson

20.   Engelbert Humperdinck

TOTAL SCORE ON SPELLING SUBTEST: _____
Enter on line (5) on page 143

Dictionary Skills

Answer Key

1. Spooky (Classics IV) |
   ("In the cool of the evening when everything is getting kind of groovy")

2. I Think We're Alone Now (Tommy James and The Shondells)
   ("Children behave, that's what they say when we're together")

3. Little Bit O' Soul (Music Explosion)
   ("Now when you're feeling low and the fish won't bite")

4. To Sir With Love (Lulu) |
   ("Those schoolgirl days of telling tales and biting nails are gone")

5. Light My Fire (The Doors)
   ("You know that it would be untrue") |

6. Bend Me, Shape Me (The American Breed)
   ("You are all the woman I need and baby you know it")

7. Somebody To Love (Jefferson Airplane)
   ("When the truth is found to be lies")

8. Friday On My Mind (The Easybeats)
   ("Monday morning feels so bad, everybody seems to nag me")

9. Lazy Day (Spanky and Our Gang)
   ("Blue sky, sunshine, what a day to talk a walk in the park")

10.   Apples, Peaches, Pumpkin Pie (Jay and The Techniques)
       ("Ready or not, here I come, gee that used to be such fun")

11.   Society's Child (Janis Ian)
       ("Come to my door, baby, face is clean and shining, black as night")

12.   (You Make Me Feel Like A) Natural Woman (Aretha Franklin)
       ("Looking out on the morning rain, I used to feel uninspired")

13.   Brown-Eyed Girl (Van Morrison)
       ("Hey where did we go, days when the rain came")

14.   Ruby Tuesday (The Rolling Stones)
       ("She would never say where she came from")

15.   Come On Down To My Boat (Every Mother's Son)
       ("She sits on the dock a fishin' in the water, uh-huh")

16.   I Can See For Miles (The Who)
       ("I know you've deceived me, now here's a surprise")

17.   Expressway To Your Heart (Soul Survivors)
       ("I've been trying to get to you for a long time")

18.   Darlin' Be Home Soon (The Lovin' Spoonful)
       ("Come and talk of all the things we did today)

19.   Don't You Care (The Buckinghams)
       ("If you don't love me, why won't you tell me")

20.   The Letter (The Boxtops)
       ("Gimme a ticket for an aeroplane")

TOTAL SCORE ON DICTIONARY SKILLS SUBTEST: _____

Enter on line (6) on page 143

Exponents

Answer Key

1. Monday Monday |
2. Mony Mony |
3. Woman Woman
4. Wonderful! Wonderful!
5. Stop Stop Stop
6. Cherry Cherry
7. Laugh Laugh
8. Liar Liar
9. Tighter, Tighter |
10. Beep Beep
11. Bang Bang
12. Iko Iko
13. Hello Hello
14. Cha Cha Cha
15. Louie Louie |
16. Um Um Um Um Um Um

17.   Shame Shame Shame

18.   Green Green

19.   Fun Fun Fun

20.   Dance Dance Dance

TOTAL SCORE ON EXPONENTS SUBTEST: _____

Enter on line (7) on page 144

Statistics

Answer Key

1. Yes, I'm Ready (Barbara Mason, #5 in 1965)

2. Hurts So Good (John Cougar, #2 in 1982)

3. There Goes My Baby (The Drifters, #2 in 1959)

4. Mercy, Mercy, Mercy (Buckinghams, #5 in 1967)

5. Oh No (The Commodores, #4 in 1981)

6. Black Is Black (Los Bravos, #4 in 1966)

7. Um, Um, Um, Um, Um, Um (Major Lance, #5 in 1964)

8. Hit The Road Jack (Ray Charles, #1 in 1961)

9. Little Bit O' Soul (Music Explosion, #2 in 1967)

10. ABC (Jackson Five, #1 in 1970)

11. Quarter To Three (Gary U.S. Bonds, #1 in 1961)

12. Tuesday Afternoon (Moody Blues, #24 in 1968)

13. Pink Cadillac (Natalie Cole, #5 in 1988)

14. You Can't Hurry Love (The Supremes, #1 in 1966)

15. Mr. Big Stuff (Jean Knight, #1 in 1971)

16. Did You Ever Have To Make Up Your Mind? (Lovin' Spoonful, #2 in 1966)

17. Oye Como Va (Santana, #13 in 1971)

18. G.T.O. (Ronny and The Daytonas, #4 in 1964)

19. Hair (The Cowsills, #2 in 1969)

20. The End (Earl Grant, #7 in 1958)

TOTAL SCORE ON STATISTICS SUBTEST: _____

Enter on line (8) on page 144

Set Theory

Answer Key

Note: Score .5 point for each correct answer.

1.	Turn! Turn! Turn!	Mr. Tambourine Man
2.	Bad Bad Leroy Brown	Time In A Bottle
3.	Hanky Panky	Crimson and Clover
4.	You've Lost That Lovin' Feelin'	(You're My) Soul and Inspiration
5.	Poor Little Fool	Travelin' Man
6.	Horse With No Name	Sister Golden Hair
7.	Soldier Boy	Will You Love Me Tomorrow?
8.	Downtown	My Love
9.	Light My Fire	Hello I Love You
10.	Will It Go Round In Circles	Nothing From Nothing
11.	Reach Out, I'll Be There	I Can't Help Myself
12.	Another One Bites The Dust	Crazy Little Thing Called Love
13.	Windy	Cherish
14.	Wedding Bell Blues	Aquarius/Let The Sunshine In
15.	Black Water	What A Fool Believes

16. Venus   Why

17. We're An American Band   The Loco-Motion

18. Love Will Keep Us Together   Do That To Me One More Time

19. Dizzy   Sheila

20. Rhinestone Cowboy   Southern Nights

NUMBER CORRECT: _____ X .5 = TOTAL
SCORE ON SET THEORY SUBTEST: _____

Enter on line (9) on page 144

Algebra

Answer Key

1. The Shoop Shoop Song

2. Judy in Disguise

3. Brandy

4. The Banana Boat Song

5. Tuesday Afternoon

6. Thank You

7. Opus 17

8. Only You

9. The Mighty Quinn

10. Money

11. A Letter From Camp

12. My Wild Beautiful Bird

13. When He Walked Me Home

14. Exordium and Terminus

15. The Ecology

16. Walking In The Sand

17.   But The Radio Rolled Me

18.   Baby I've Been Thinking

19.   Soulsville, U.S.A

20.   Of My Baby's Love

TOTAL SCORE ON ALGEBRA SUBTEST: _____

Enter on line (10) on page 144

Finance

Answer Key

1. Dime
2. A dollar and a half
3. A million dollars
4. A quarter
5. $14.27
6. Forty cents
7. Nickel
8. Thousand dollar
9. Fifty dollars
10. Dollar
11. Fifteen cents
12. A penny
13. A hundred
14. Fifty cents
15. Twenty
16. $2.50

17. Penny

18. Nickel

19. Eleven dollar

20. Ten

TOTAL SCORE ON FINANCE SUBTEST: _____
Enter on line (11) on page 144

Addition

Answer Key

1. The Pips

2. The Cavaliers

3. The All Stars

4. His Blue Caps

5. The Pharaohs

6. The Detroit Wheels

7. The Stone Canyon Band

8. The Mindbenders

9. The Shondells

10. The Playboys

11. Billy Ward

12. Gary Puckett

13. Bob Seger

14. Jimmy Gilmer

15. Bo Donaldson

16. Hank Ballard

17.   Tony Orlando

18.   Sergio Mendes

19.   Link Wray

20.   Frankie Lymon

TOTAL SCORE ON ADDITION SUBTEST: _____

Enter on line (12) on page 144

U.S. Geography

Answer Key

1. Boston

2. Winslow (Arizona)

3. Galveston

4. New York

5. Houston

6. Chicago

7. Savannah

8. Little Rock

9. Chicago

10. Memphis

11. Miami

12. Pittsburgh

13. Memphis

14. Indianapolis

15. L.A.

16. Seattle

17.   New Orleans

18.   By The Time I Get To Phoenix

19.   Wichita Lineman

20.   Galveston

TOTAL SCORE ON U.S. GEOGRAPHY SUBTEST: _____

Enter on line (13) on page 145

British History

Answer Key

1. I Should Have Known Better
2. Ticket To Ride
3. Eleanor Rigby
4. Nowhere Man
5. I've Just Seen A Face
6. She Loves You
7. The Ballad of John and Yoko
8. Do You Want To Know A Secret?
9. Something
10. Little Child
11. She Came In Through The Bathroom Window
12. You Never Give Me Your Money
13. Anytime At All
14. Lady Madonna
15. The Fool On The Hill
16. It's Only Love

17. A Hard Day's Night

18. Magical Mystery Tour

19. Blackbird

20. The End

TOTAL SCORE ON BRITISH HISTORY SUBTEST: _____
Enter on line (14) on page 145

Black History

Answer Key

1. ABC (The Jackson Five)

2. Bernadette (The Four Tops)

3. Come and Get These Memories (Martha and The Vandellas)

4. Don't Mess With Bill (The Marvelettes)

5. Every Little Bit Hurts (Brenda Holloway)

6. For Once In My Life (Stevie Wonder)

7. Going To A Go-Go (The Miracles)

8. Heat Wave (Martha and The Vandellas)

9. I Heard It Through The Grapevine (Marvin Gaye / Gladys Knight and The Pips)

10. Just My Imagination (The Temptations)

11. Keep On Truckin' (Eddie Kendricks)

12. The Love You Save (The Jackson Five)

13. My Guy (Mary Wells)

14. Nothing But Heartaches (The Supremes)

15. Ooo Baby Baby (The Miracles)

16.   Pride and Joy (Marvin Gaye)

17.   Quicksand (Martha and The Vandellas)

18.   Road Runner (Jr. Walker and The All Stars)

19.   Sail On (The Commodores)

20.   This Old Heart Of Mine (The Isley Brothers)

TOTAL SCORE ON BLACK HISTORY SUBTEST: _____

Enter on line (15) on page 145

Religion

Answer Key

1. Paul Anka

2. Andy Gibb

3. Rick Springfield

4. Bobby Rydell

5. James Darren

6. Bobby Sherman

7. David Cassidy

8. Michael Jackson

9. Bobby Darin

10. Donny Osmond

11. Bobby Vinton

12. Dion

13. Fabian

14. Rick Nelson

15. Paul Petersen

16. Peter Frampton

17.   Bobby Vee

18.   Elvis Presley

19.   Shaun Cassidy

20.   Frankie Avalon

TOTAL SCORE ON RELIGION SUBTEST: _____

Enter on line (16) on page 145

Psychology

Answer Key

1. Lovin' You (Minnie Riperton)

2. I Think I Love You (The Partridge Family)

3. One Bad Apple (The Osmonds)

4. The Candy Man (Sammy Davis Jr.)

5. Kung-Fu Fighting (Carl Douglas)

6. Thank God I'm A Country Boy (John Denver)

7. Afternoon Delight (Starland Vocal Band)

8. You Light Up My Life (Debbie Boone)

9. Delta Dawn (Helen Reddy)

10. Convoy (C.W. McCall)

11. Everything Is Beautiful (Ray Stevens)

12. Tie A Yellow Ribbon (Tony Orlando and Dawn)

13. You're Havin' My Baby (Paul Anka)

14. Mandy (Barry Manilow)

15. Baby Don't Get Hooked On Me (Mac Davis)

16. My Ding A Ling (Chuck Berry)

17.   Close To You (The Carpenters)

18.   Cracklin' Rosie (Neil Diamond)

19.   Love Will Keep Us Together (The Captain and Tennille)

20.   Seasons In The Sun (Terry Jacks)

TOTAL SCORE ON PSYCHOLOGY SUBTEST: _____

Enter on line (17) on page 145

Counterculture

Answer Key

1. The Eve of Destruction (Barry McGuire)

2. Ohio (Crosby, Stills, Nash and Young)

3. Get Together (The Youngbloods)

4. Peace Train (Cat Stevens)

5. Scarborough Fair / Canticle (Simon and Garfunkel)

6. Sweet Cherry Wine (Tommy James and The Shondells)

7. Turn! Turn! Turn! (The Byrds)

8. Day Is Done (Peter, Paul and Mary)

9. Abraham, Martin and John (Dion)

10. Fortunate Son (Creedence Clearwater Revival)

11. Yellow River (Christie)

12. Blowin' In The Wind (Bob Dylan / Peter, Paul and Mary)

13. What's Going On? (Marvin Gaye)

14. The Times They Are A-Changing (Bob Dylan)

15. Ball Of Confusion (The Temptations)

16. People Got To Be Free (The Rascals)

17. Lay Down (Candles in the Rain) (Melanie with the Edwin Hawkins Singers)

18. Sky Pilot (Eric Burden and The Animals)

19. Revolution (The Beatles)

20. For What It's Worth (Buffalo Springfield)

TOTAL SCORE ON COUNTERCULTURE SUBTEST: _____

Enter on line (18) on page 145

Zoology

Answer Key

1. Mockingbird

2. Me and You and a Dog Named Boo

3. The Monkey Time

4. Nashville Cats

5. White Rabbit

6. Cat's In The Cradle

7. Wild Horses

8. Rockin' Robin

9. Fly Like An Eagle

10. Muskrat Love

11. What's New Pussycat?

12. Free Bird

13. Funky Worm

14. Dark Horse

15. Year Of The Cat

16. Cat Scratch Fever

17. A Horse With No Name

18. Elusive Butterfly

19. Honky Cat

20. Crocodile Rock

TOTAL SCORE ON ZOOLOGY SUBTEST: _____

Enter on line (19) on page 146

Pre-med

Answer Key

1. Poison Ivy

2. Fever

3. Classical Gas

4. Hit Me With Your Best Shot

5. Needles and Pins

6. Dust In The Wind

7. Working In The Coal Mine

8. Turn! Turn! Turn!

9. Two Faces Have I

10. Cat Scratch Fever

11. Nineteenth Nervous Breakdown

12. Blinded By The Light

13. You Can't Sit Down

14. Havin' My Baby

15. Sleepwalk

16. Shaking All Over

17.   Beans In My Ears

18.   Dizzy

19.   Rockin' Pneumonia and The Boogie Woogie Flu

20.   Heart Attack

TOTAL SCORE ON PRE-MED SUBTEST: _____

Enter on line (20) on page 146

Evolution

Answer Key

1. Four

2. Five o'clock

3. At eight

4. Six o'clock

5. Five o'clock

6. Three

7. Five o'clock

8. Four o'clock

9. Nine o'clock

10. 10:05

11. Nine To Five (Dolly Parton)

12. Five O'Clock World (The Vogues)

13. Midnight Confessions (The Grassroots)

14. Quarter To Three (Gary U.S. Bonds)

15. In The Midnight Hour (Wilson Pickett)

16. 25 Or 6 To Four (Chicago)

17. Midnight Blue (Melissa Manchester)

18. Twelve Thirty (The Mamas and The Papas)

19. Six O'Clock (The Lovin' Spoonful)

20. Midnight At The Oasis (Maria Muldaur)

TOTAL SCORE ON EVOLUTION SUBTEST: _____
Enter on line (21) on page 146

Chemistry

Answer Key

1. To Sir With Love

2. The Chapel of Love

3. Jungle Love

4. Modern Love

5. Somebody To Love

6. The Best of My Love

7. Never My Love

8. Sunshine of Your Love

9. Standing in the Shadows of Love

10. Walk Away From Love

11. He's Sure The Boy I Love

12. Whole Lotta Love

13. What the World Needs Now is Love

14. Lawyers in Love

15. Teenager In Love

16. World Without Love

17.   For Your Love

18.   Bye Bye Love

19.   Words of Love

20.   Dedicated To The One I Love

TOTAL SCORE ON CHEMISTRY SUBTEST: _____

Enter on line (22) on page 146

Human Physiology

Answer Key

1. Smoke Gets In Your Eyes

2. Over My Head

3. Sunshine On My Shoulders

4. The First Time Ever I Saw Your Face

5. Doctor My Eyes

6. Slow Hand

7. Take Me In Your Arms

8. Skinny Legs and All

9. Baby Scratch My Back

10. Can't Get It Out Of My Head

11. Suite: Judy Blue Eyes

12. Your Nose Is Gonna Grow

13. Your Smiling Face

14. Goin' Out Of My Head

15. Temptation Eyes

16. Two Faces Have I

17.   Ebony Eyes

18.   Head Games

19.   Legs

20.   Tush

TOTAL SCORE ON HUMAN PHYSIOLOGY SUBTEST: _____
Enter on line (23) on page 146

The Scientific Method

Answer Key

1. Do You Know The Way To San Jose?

2. Does Anybody Really Know What Time It Is?

3. Will You Love Me Tomorrow?

4. Where Have All The Flowers Gone?

5. Do You Want To Dance?

6. Is She Really Going Out With Him?

7. How Can You Mend A Broken Heart?

8. Have I The Right?

9. Does Your Chewing Gum Lose Its Flavor (On The Bedpost Over Night)?

10. Who'll Stop The Rain?

11. Do Ya Think I'm Sexy?

12. Where's The Playground, Susie?

13. Do You Want To Know A Secret?

14. Have You Seen Your Mother, Baby, Standing In The Shadow?

15. Will It Go Round In Circles?

16.   Why Do Fools Fall In Love?

17.   Wouldn't It Be Nice?

18.   Did You Ever Have To Make Up Your Mind?

19.   Don't You Care?

20.   Is That All There Is?

TOTAL SCORE ON SCIENTIFIC METHOD SUBTEST: _____

Enter on line (24) on page 146

Fine Arts

Answer Key

1.   Cream
2.   Big Brother and the Holding Company
3.   Billy Joel
4.   Pink Floyd
5.   The Mamas and The Papas
6.   The Grateful Dead
7.   Cat Stevens
8.   The Beach Boys
9.   The Rolling Stones
10.   Fleetwood Mac
11.   The Moody Blues
12.   Bruce Springsteen
13.   Bob Dylan
14.   Herb Alpert and The Tijuana Brass
15.   Elton John
16.   Joni Mitchell

17.   Stevie Wonder

18.   Crosby, Stills, Nash and Young

19.   Eric Clapton

20.   Yes

TOTAL SCORE ON FINE ARTS SUBTEST: _____
Enter on line (25) on page 147

Authors

Answer Key

1. Carole King

2. Gene Pitney

3. Laura Nyro

4. Willie Nelson

5. Neil Sedaka

6. Jackie DeShannon

7. Smokey Robinson

8. Neil Diamond

9. Bob Dylan

10. Joe South

11. Paul Anka

12. John D. Loudermilk

13. Otis Redding

14. Paul McCartney

15. Leon Russell

16. Mac Davis

17.   Kris Kristofferson

18.   Bruce Springsteen

19.   Isaac Hayes

20.   The Isley Brothers

TOTAL SCORE ON AUTHORS SUBTEST: _____

Enter on line (26) on page 147

Dance

Answer Key

1.	Wah-Wahtusi	K.	The Orlons
2.	The Peppermint Twist	I.	Joey Dee and The Starlighters
3.	The Jerk	B.	The Larks
4.	C'mon and Swim	N.	Bobby Freeman
5.	Do The Freddie	Q.	Freddie and The Dreamers
6.	The Bristol Stomp	E.	The Dovells
7.	Mashed Potato Time	C.	Dee Dee Sharp
8.	Boogaloo Down Broadway	G.	Fantastic Johnny C
9.	The Hustle	M.	Van McCoy
10.	The Alley Cat	F.	Bent Fabric and His Piano
11.	Shimmy Shimmy Ko-Ko-Bop	P.	Little Anthony and The Imperials
12.	Monkey Time	R.	Major Lance
13.	(Do The) Funky Chicken	A.	Rufus Thomas

14.   The Cha-Cha-Cha   O.   Bobby Rydell

15.   Pony Time   J.   Chubby Checker

16.   The Monster Mash   H.   Bobby "Boris" Pickett

17.   Beer Barrel Polka   L.   Bobby Vinton

18.   The Stroll   D.   The Diamonds

19.   Little Eva

20.   Grand Funk

TOTAL SCORE ON DANCE SUBTEST: _____

Enter on line (27) on page 147

The Grand Masters

Answer Key

1.   James Brown

2.   Johnny Cash

3.   Jim Morrison

4.   Eric Clapton

5.   Jackie Wilson

6.   Louis Armstrong

7.   Bobby Bland

8.   Aretha Franklin

9.   Janis Joplin

10. Jerry Butler (inducted as a member of The Impressions)

11. Jerry Lee Lewis

12. Bruce Springsteen

13. Elvis Presley

14. Roy Orbison

15. Ray Charles

16. Lloyd Price

17.   Wilson Pickett

18.   Michael Jackson (inducted as a member of The Jackson Five)

19.   Sam Cooke

20.   Fats Domino

TOTAL SCORE ON THE GRAND MASTERS SUBTEST: _____

Enter on line (28) on page 147

Film

Answer Key

1. Led Zeppelin
2. Bob Dylan
3. David Bowie
4. The Rolling Stones
5. Herman's Hermits
6. Dave Clark Five
7. The Monkees
8. The Village People
9. The Who
10. The Band
11. Butch Cassidy and The Sundance Kid
12. The Poseidon Adventure
13. The Sterile Cuckoo
14. Midnight Cowboy
15. Lovers and Other Strangers
16. The Graduate

17.   Nashville

18.   Saturday Night Fever

19.   Grease

20.   Thank God It's Friday

TOTAL SCORE ON FILM SUBTEST: _____

Enter on line (29) on page 147

Comedy

Answer Key

1. Short People (Randy Newman)

2. Hello Muddah, Hello Faddah (Allan Sherman)

3. They're Coming To Take Me Away Ha Ha! (Napoleon XIV)

4. A Boy Named Sue (Johnny Cash)

5. Purple People Eater (Sheb Wooley)

6. King Tut (Steve Martin)

7. Troglodyte (Cave Man) (Jimmy Castor Bunch)

8. Leader Of The Laundromat (The Detergents)

9. Mr. Custer (Larry Verne)

10. Gitarzan (Ray Stevens)

11. The Monster Mash (Bobby "Boris" Pickett and The Cryptkickers)

12. Transfusion (Nervous Norvus)

13. Along Came Jones (The Coasters)

14. The Return of the Red Baron (The Royal Guardsmen)

15. Cheeseburger in Paradise (Jimmy Buffett)

16.   The Ballad of Irving (Frank Gallop)

17.   Dead Skunk (Loudon Wainwright III)

18.   Alley-Oop (The Hollywood Argyles)

19.   Convoy (C.W. McCall)

20.   Kookie Kookie (Lend Me Your Comb) (Edward Byrnes and Connie Stevens)

TOTAL SCORE ON COMEDY SUBTEST: _____

Enter on line (30) on page 147

Calculation of Final Score

ADD ALL LANGUAGE ARTS SUBTEST SCORES

FOREIGN LANGUAGE   (1)_____

JOURNALISM   (2)_____

GRAMMAR   (3)_____

PUBLIC SPEAKING   (4)_____

SPELLING   (5)_____

DICTIONARY SKILLS   (6)_____

LANGUAGE ARTS TOTAL:_____

enter on line (A)
on pg. 148

ADD ALL MATHEMATICS SUBTEST SCORES

EXPONENTS	(7)	_____
STATISTICS	(8)	_____
SET THEORY	(9)	_____
ALGEBRA	(10)	_____
FINANCE	(11)	_____
ADDITION	(12)	_____

MATHEMATICS TOTAL:_____

enter on line (B)
on pg. 148

ADD ALL SOCIAL STUDIES SUBTEST SCORES

U.S. GEOGRAPHY   (13)   _____

BRITISH HISTORY   (14)   _____

BLACK HISTORY   (15)   _____

RELIGION   (16)   _____

PSYCHOLOGY   (17)   _____

COUNTERCULTURE   (18)   _____

SOCIAL STUDIES TOTAL:_____

enter on line (C)
on pg. 148

ADD ALL SCIENCE SUBTEST SCORES

ZOOLOGY   (19)   _____

PRE-MED   (20)   _____

EVOLUTION   (21)   _____

CHEMISTRY   (22)   _____

HUMAN PHYSIOLOGY   (23)   _____

SCIENTIFIC METHOD   (24)   _____

SCIENCE TOTAL:_____
enter on line (D)
on pg. 148

ADD ALL ARTS SUBTEST SCORES

FINE ARTS   (25)   _____

AUTHORS   (26)   _____

DANCE   (27)   _____

THE GRAND MASTERS   (28)   _____

FILM   (29)   _____

COMEDY   (30)   _____

ARTS TOTAL:_____
enter on line (E)
on pg. 148

ADD ALL TEST TOTALS

LANGUAGE ARTS TOTAL   (A)   _____

MATHEMATICS TOTAL   (B)   _____

SCIENCE TOTAL   (C)   _____

SOCIAL STUDIES TOTAL   (D)   _____

ARTS TOTAL   (E)   _____

Subtotal: ADD (A) THROUGH (E)_____
All standardized tests spot you 200 points just for showing up, so add 200 points just for buying the book:

+200

FINAL SCORE_____
See next page for a ranking of your score.

Final Score Interpretation

750-800: Simply perfect! You are officially a Fifth Beatle!

700-749: Quite Incredible...You must have grown up with a transistor radio surgically attached to your ear.

650-699: Most Excellent...You have our endorsement for a Vice-Presidency with ASCAP.

600-649: High Praise...Perhaps you'd like to consult when I write the next edition?

550-599: Very Good...Tell me, does your stereo ever overheat?

500-549: Good...You really know your music, and are probably starting to treat the next generation like your parents treated you!

450-499: Respectable...The ones you forgot probably meant you had a good time in the Sixties!

400-449: Adequate...And I take great pride in the fact that you're probably cursed with some of these songs stuck in your head.

350-399: Passing...Were you doing homework when you should have been watching "American Bandstand"?

300-349: Marginal...You should crank up more oldies stations and give MTV a break!

250-299:   Brush Up...You probably think Abbie Hoffman is an advice columnist, and Ringo Starr is a constellation.

200-249:   Vast Improvement Needed..."Alan Freed" is *not* a headline about a parole decision.

About the Author

Barb is a veteran of writing and hosting trivia games with a twist. On America Online, "Classic Rock Jukebox," her acclaimed weekly chat room game and "Rock Around The Clock," her daily dose of irreverent rock 'n roll mind-benders, have amused and challenged her devoted players since 1994.

She lives in New Jersey with her incredibly patient and loving husband Jerry and their sons Jordan and David, who now know better than to ask their mom who John Lennon was while being held captive on a two-hour car ride.

Printed in the United States
136993LV00002B/77/A